Break Every Chain

Freedom From All Addictions

The 100 Day Re-Program

Karajah Yashar

BLACKSTONE PUBLISHING

Orlando, FL

www.BSPBooks.com

Copyright © 2024 by Blackstone Publishing

ISBN: 978-1-962691-37-6

First Edition: July 2024

Table of Contents

The Break Every Chain Prayer

Heavenly Father,

We come before You today, humbly seeking Your presence and Your power. Lord, we acknowledge that addiction has a strong hold over our lives, and we know that only through Your grace and mercy can we break free from its chains.

In the name of Jesus, we ask for Your divine intervention. Break every chain of addiction that binds us. Release us from the grips of substances, behaviors, and patterns that have taken control of our lives. We declare that Your power is greater than any addiction, and through Your strength, we can overcome.

Lord, renew our minds and our spirits. Give us the courage to face our struggles and the wisdom to seek help when we need it. Surround us with a support system that reflects Your love and encourages our journey toward healing and recovery.

We pray for the strength to resist temptation and to make choices that honor You. Fill us with Your Holy Spirit, guiding us in every step we take. Help us to find our identity and worth in You, and not in the things that have enslaved us.

Father, we place our trust in You. We know that through Jesus Christ, we are more than conquerors. We claim victory over addiction in His holy name, knowing that You are with us every step of the way.

Thank You, Lord, for Your unfailing love and Your unending grace. We give You all the glory and praise, now and forever.

In Jesus' mighty name, we pray.

Amen.

How to Use This Book

The "Break Every Chain" program is structured as a 100-day journey, divided into four sections. The first ten days focus on planning, where you will read the information and mentally prepare for the exercises. From day 10 to day 50, you will engage in the first round of execution, applying the strategies and steps outlined in the book. Days 50 to 55 are dedicated to review, allowing you to reflect on your progress and adjust your approach as needed. From day 55 to day 95, you will begin the second round of execution, refining and reinforcing your practices. Finally, days 95 to 100 are set aside for a final review, assessing your achievements and solidifying your commitment to a life free from addiction.

While this workbook can be completed alone, it is recommended that you work through it in collaboration with a group, whether it's your own circle of trusted friends and family or a "Break Every Chain" support group. Support is a crucial element in overcoming addiction, providing encouragement, accountability, and shared experiences that can bolster your resolve. Fighting your battles in isolation can be counterproductive, as secrecy and isolation can weaken your resolve and intensify your struggles. Utilizing a positive support network fosters connection and mutual support, making overcoming addiction more achievable. Remember, you are not alone in this fight, and together with God and a supportive community, you can break every chain and reclaim your life.

The First 10 Days

The first ten days of the "Break Every Chain" program are dedicated to the planning stage. During this crucial period, you will immerse yourself in reading and understanding the information provided for the eighteen exercises. This initial phase is not about diving into the physical execution of the exercises but about equipping yourself with the knowledge and insights necessary to approach each exercise with confidence and clarity. You should notify your support network of your impending 100 day journey and prepare them for the part they will play. By thoroughly reviewing the material, you will build a solid foundation for the practical application that follows.

As you absorb the details of each exercise, begin to craft a personalized plan that aligns with your unique needs and circumstances. Consider the logistics of how you will integrate these exercises into your daily routine. Think about the time of day that would be most conducive to practice, the environment that would best support your efforts, and any tools or resources you might need. This planning stage is an opportunity to anticipate potential challenges and devise strategies to overcome them, ensuring a smoother execution when you commence the exercises.

Mental preparation is a key component of these ten days. Visualize yourself performing each exercise successfully, reinforcing a positive and determined mindset. Picture the steps you will take, the feelings of accomplishment you will experience, and the growth you will achieve. This mental rehearsal will help to alleviate any anxieties or uncertainties you might have, building your confidence and commitment. By the end of this planning stage, you will be mentally and strategically prepared to embark on the exercises with a clear vision and a motivated spirit, setting the stage for a transformative journey.

You have 10 Days to fully read and fill out pages 8-44. Give yourself time each day to work on it. Reflect on how you will achieve the exercises.

Start Date: _____

Date 10 Days from Start Date: _____

My Profile Page

Personal Information

Full Name: _____

My Immediate Support
(Check in with Your supports weekly during this program)

#1

Full Name: _____

Relationship: _____

Contact Number: _____

#2

Full Name: _____

Relationship: _____

Contact Number: _____

#3

Full Name: _____

Relationship: _____

Contact Number: _____

I Will Utilize My Supports to Better Myself!

*Document Calls with the Call Log on Pages 75-94

Addiction Information

- **Type of Addiction(s):** (Select all that apply)
    - ☐ Alcohol
    - ☐ Drugs (Specify: _____)
    - ☐ Nicotine
    - ☐ Gambling
    - ☐ Internet/Social Media
    - ☐ Gaming
    - ☐ Shopping
    - ☐ Sex
    - ☐ Pornography
    - ☐ Food
    - ☐ Sugar/ Salt
    - ☐ Other (Specify: _____)
    -
- **Duration of Addiction:** _____

    _____

- **Frequency of Addiction:** _____

    _____

Previous Treatment/Programs Attended:

- ☐ Counseling
- ☐ Rehabilitation Center
- ☐ Support Groups
- ☐ Medical Treatment
- ☐ Other (Specify: _____)
- ☐ None

Recovery Goals

- **Short-term Goals:**
  -
    1. _____
  -
    2. _____
  -
    3. _____

- **Long-term Goals:**
  -
    1. _____
  -
    2. _____
  -
    3. _____

Support System

- **Family Support:**
  - ☐ Yes
  - ☐ No
  - ☐ Limited
- **Friends Support:**
  - ☐ Yes
  - ☐ No
  - ☐ Limited
- **Support Group Attendance:**
  - ☐ Yes (Specify: _____)
  - ☐ No

Personal Interests and Hobbies

- _____

- _____

- _____

Availability

- **Preferred Meeting Days:**
  - ☐ Monday
  - ☐ Tuesday
  - ☐ Wednesday
  - ☐ Thursday
  - ☐ Friday
  - ☐ Saturday
  - ☐ Sunday
- **Preferred Meeting Times:**
  - ☐ Morning
  - ☐ Afternoon
  - ☐ Evening

Additional Notes

- _____

- _____

- _____

_____

Signature: _____

Date: _____

Did You Know?

Almost everybody has some form of addiction, whether it's a mild habit or a severe dependency. Some people's addictions may be relatively benign, such as an attachment to social media or a penchant for sugary snacks, leading to repercussions like reduced productivity or weight gain. In contrast, others face extremely detrimental addictions to substances like drugs or alcohol, which can lead to devastating consequences such as imprisonment or even death. Despite the varying degrees of severity, all addictions have the potential to impede personal growth and well-being.

Addictions, regardless of their nature, keep people from being the best version of themselves. They cloud judgment, sap motivation, and divert focus from meaningful pursuits and relationships. Whether it's an addiction to work, shopping, gaming, or more destructive substances, these habits create barriers to living a fulfilling and balanced life. The constant need to satisfy an addiction can erode self-esteem and lead to feelings of guilt and shame, further entrenching the harmful cycle. By addressing and overcoming these addictions, individuals can reclaim their lives and redirect their energy toward positive and productive endeavors.

Breaking the chain of addiction is crucial in overcoming these bad habits and becoming our best selves. This process involves acknowledging the problem, seeking help, and committing to change. It often requires a multifaceted approach, including deliverance through the Holy Spirit, support from loved ones, professional counseling, and developing healthier coping mechanisms. By breaking free from the grip of addiction, individuals can unlock their potential, improve their physical and mental health, and build stronger, more meaningful connections with others. Ultimately, overcoming addiction is a vital step towards achieving personal growth and living a life of purpose and fulfillment.

Break Every Chain: The Urgency of Overcoming Addiction

Addiction, in all its forms, is a devastating force that can infiltrate every aspect of our lives. Whether stemming from spiritual strongholds, deeply ingrained mental/ emotional programming, or physical dependency, addiction exerts a powerful influence that can dominate and control our thoughts, emotions, and behaviors. It strips away our rational judgment, leading us down a path of self-sabotage and potentially isolation. The grip of addiction undermines our relationships, aspirations, and overall well-being, making it imperative to confront and overcome.

Regardless of its origin, overcoming addiction requires a profound commitment to cleansing and renewal of mind, body, and spirit. This journey is not merely about breaking free from harmful habits; it entails a holistic transformation aimed at reclaiming one's sense of self and purpose. It involves confronting the underlying issues that fuel addiction, whether they be emotional pain, trauma, or unmet spiritual needs. The process demands resilience and perseverance in the face of setbacks and challenges, yet the promise of liberation and restored health makes every effort worthwhile.

The path to freedom from addiction is fraught with obstacles, but the rewards are immense. Achieving sobriety and reclaiming control over one's life brings not only personal fulfillment but also restores relationships and opens the door to new possibilities. It requires a willingness to seek help, confront difficult truths, and embrace change. Through dedication to healing the mind, adopting healthier habits, and nurturing spiritual well-being, individuals can break free from the chains of addiction and embark on a journey toward lasting recovery and renewed vitality.

Understanding Addiction and Recognizing Its Signs

Addiction is a complex condition characterized by a compulsive engagement in rewarding stimuli, despite adverse consequences. It can manifest in various forms, including substance dependence (such as drugs, alcohol, and nicotine) and behavioral addictions (like gambling, shopping, internet use, and gaming). At its core, addiction is not just a matter of frequent use or engagement but involves a psychological and physiological dependence that significantly impacts an individual's life.

Addiction develops through a combination of genetic, environmental, and psychological factors. The brain's reward system plays a crucial role, where the release of dopamine creates pleasurable sensations, reinforcing the behavior. Over time, the brain adapts, leading to tolerance (requiring more of the substance or behavior to achieve the same effect) and withdrawal symptoms when the substance or behavior is not available. This cycle of seeking and relief creates a powerful grip that can be challenging to break.

One of the first steps in addressing addiction is recognizing its presence. Many people struggling with addiction may be in denial, making it essential to understand the signs and symptoms that indicate a problem. Here are several key indicators:

1. **Loss of Control**: An inability to limit the intake of a substance or engagement in a behavior. Despite wanting to stop or reduce use, the individual finds themselves repeatedly returning to it.
2. **Neglecting Responsibilities**: Addiction often leads to neglect of daily responsibilities at work, school, or home. An individual may miss important events, fail to meet deadlines, disregard financial responsibilities, or neglect household chores due to their preoccupation with the addictive substance or activity.

14

3. **Continued Use Despite Harm**: Persisting in the behavior despite knowing it causes physical, emotional, or social harm. This could include health issues, strained relationships, legal problems, or financial difficulties.
4. **Tolerance and Withdrawal**: Developing a tolerance, meaning needing more of the substance or behavior to achieve the desired effect, and experiencing withdrawal symptoms when trying to stop. Withdrawal can manifest as physical symptoms (like shaking, sweating, nausea) or psychological symptoms (such as anxiety, depression, irritability).
5. **Loss of Interest in Other Activities**: An individual may lose interest in activities they once enjoyed, dedicating more time and energy to the addictive behavior. Hobbies, social interactions, and other interests fall by the wayside.
6. **Secrecy and Isolation**: Individuals may become secretive about their behavior, going to great lengths to hide it from family and friends. They might also isolate themselves, avoiding social situations where the addictive behavior is not possible or could be discovered.
7. **Escalation**: Increasing the frequency or intensity of the behavior over time. For instance, someone might start with occasional gambling but gradually progress to more frequent and higher-stakes betting.

Recognizing these signs is the first step towards seeking help and initiating recovery. It is important to approach the subject with compassion and understanding, whether you are recognizing these signs in yourself or in someone you care about. Addiction is a medical condition, not a moral failing, and addressing it requires support, treatment, and a commitment to change.

The Stranglehold of Addiction

"Be sober, be vigilant; because your adversary the devil, as a roaring lion, walketh about, seeking whom he may devour"
1 Peter 5:8

Addiction can weaken our defenses and make us vulnerable to spiritual attacks. Therefore, maintaining sobriety is not just about physical abstinence but also about cultivating a clear and focused mind that is resilient against the schemes of the enemy. By staying rooted in prayer, scripture, and community support, we can fortify our spiritual defenses and uphold a sober lifestyle that honors God and protects our well-being. The deceptive nature of addiction distorts our priorities, leading us to prioritize the substance or behavior over all else. It blinds us to the consequences of our actions, fostering destructive behaviors that harm ourselves and those we care about. What begins as a coping mechanism or a source of temporary relief can quickly spiral into a consuming obsession, reshaping our daily lives and distorting our sense of identity and purpose.

Overcoming addiction requires a courageous confrontation of these distorted beliefs and behaviors. It demands a willingness to acknowledge the impact of addiction on our lives and the lives of others, and to take decisive steps towards recovery. Breaking free from addiction involves reclaiming control over our thoughts and actions, rebuilding relationships, and rediscovering a sense of purpose beyond the grip of dependency. Through support, self-reflection, and a commitment to healing, individuals can begin to unravel addiction's hold and forge a path toward renewed health, stability, and emotional well-being.

Spiritual Strongholds

"Submit yourselves therefore to God. Resist the devil, and he will flee from you." James 4:7

Spiritual strongholds represent various unseen entities that sustain addiction, often rooted in generational curses and exacerbated by the presence of negative serpent spirits. The spirit world is real. These strongholds may manifest as feelings of worthlessness, shame, or guilt, perpetuated by the addictive behavior itself and inherited patterns of dysfunction within families. Generational curses, passed down through familial lines, can contribute to a predisposition towards addiction, creating a spiritual and psychological framework that makes breaking free even more challenging. These curses often involve unresolved traumas, destructive behaviors, and patterns of thinking that reinforce addictive tendencies across generations.

Overcoming these spiritual strongholds necessitates a comprehensive approach to spiritual renewal and reclaiming inherent worth and purpose. It involves confronting and dismantling the lies and distortions imposed by addiction and generational curses, replacing them with spiritual truths that affirm individual identity and divine purpose. Spiritual renewal includes engaging in prayer, meditation, and seeking guidance from spiritual mentors or counselors who can provide insight and support in navigating the complexities of addiction and spiritual warfare.

Recognizing the influence of serpent spirits is also crucial in breaking spiritual strongholds associated with addiction. These spiritual entities may exploit vulnerabilities and exacerbate addictive behaviors by fostering feelings of hopelessness, despair, and self-destructive impulses. Addressing these influences requires spiritual discernment and warfare, engaging in spiritual practices such as deliverance prayers, renouncing generational curses, and seeking the intervention of spiritual authorities within faith communities.

By embracing a holistic approach to spiritual healing, individuals can begin to dismantle the spiritual strongholds that perpetuate addiction. This journey involves not only personal introspection and healing but also a commitment to breaking free from inherited patterns of dysfunction and spiritual oppression. Through faith, perseverance, and the support of a nurturing community, individuals can reclaim their spiritual identity, break the chains of addiction, and embark on a path of lasting recovery and spiritual freedom.

Practices such as prayer and meditation are powerful tools in fostering spiritual renewal. Prayer allows individuals to communicate with God through Christ, seeking guidance, strength, and forgiveness. It serves as a reminder that we are not alone in our struggles and that divine support is always available. Meditation, on the other hand, helps cultivate inner peace and mindfulness, enabling individuals to listen to God, and focus on the present moment quieting the chaos within our minds. Together, these practices can provide a solid foundation for spiritual growth and resilience.

Participation in faith-based communities also plays a crucial role in breaking spiritual strongholds. These communities offer a network of support, encouragement, and accountability. Being part of a group that shares common values and beliefs can reinforce an individual's commitment to recovery. Additionally, the shared experiences and wisdom within these communities can provide valuable insights and coping strategies. Faith-based gatherings, worship services, and fellowship activities create a sense of belonging and purpose, which are vital in maintaining long-term sobriety.

Mental Programming

"And be not conformed to this world: but be ye transformed by the renewing of your mind, that ye may prove what is that good, and acceptable, and perfect, will of God." Romans 12:2

Mental programming is the intricate network of habitual thought patterns and behaviors that sustain addiction, often encompassing negative self-talk, denial, and rationalization of harmful behaviors. These patterns reinforce the addictive cycle, fostering a distorted perception of reality and undermining efforts toward recovery. Breaking free from this mental stronghold requires a deliberate and sustained effort to recondition the mind.

Renewing our minds is a transformative process emphasized in Romans 12:2. This biblical principle underscores the importance of replacing destructive thoughts with positive, empowering ones aligned with God's will. By immersing ourselves in scripture, prayer, and positive affirmations, we can cultivate a mindset that promotes healing, resilience, and clarity of purpose.

Reprogramming the mind involves challenging and changing deeply ingrained beliefs that contribute to addictive behaviors. It requires mindfulness and self-awareness to recognize and challenge negative thought patterns as they arise. Cognitive-behavioral techniques, coupled with spiritual practices such as meditation and fellowship with supportive communities, provide effective tools for breaking the cycle of addiction. By committing to this process of mental renewal, individuals can gain control over their thoughts and behaviors, paving the way for sustained recovery and a renewed sense of hope and purpose.

2 Corinthians 5:17 reminds us, "Therefore if any man be in Christ, he is a new creature: old things are passed away; behold, all things are become new." This powerful declaration

underscores the transformative power of faith in Christ. By accepting Jesus into our lives and surrendering to His will, we become new creatures, free from the bondage of addiction. This spiritual renewal is essential for breaking the mental chains of addiction and embracing a life of freedom and purpose.

Positive affirmations grounded in biblical truth are another powerful tool in reprogramming thought patterns. Scripture provides a wealth of affirmations that can counteract negative self-talk and build self-esteem. By consistently affirming our worth, strength, and ability to overcome addiction through Christ, we can create a more positive and empowering internal dialogue. Philippians 4:13, "I can do all things through Christ which strengtheneth me," serves as a potent reminder of the divine strength available to us. This shift in mindset, rooted in faith, not only helps to weaken the hold of addiction but also fosters a greater sense of self-efficacy and resilience. Through the combined use of biblical guidance, prayer, and positive affirmations, we can renew our minds and pave the way for lasting recovery.

Physical Dependency

"If any man defile the temple of God, him shall God destroy;
for the temple of God is holy, which temple ye are."
1 Corinthians 3:17

Physical dependency is the body's reliance on a substance or activity to function normally. This type of dependency occurs when the body adapts to the presence of the substance, integrating it into its regular processes. When the substance is not available, the body experiences withdrawal symptoms, which can range from mild discomfort to severe physical and psychological distress. This dependency creates a powerful cycle where the body demands the substance to maintain equilibrium, making it difficult to quit without experiencing significant discomfort.

Overcoming physical dependency requires a commitment to health and wellness. Addiction often leads to a deterioration of physical health, making the body reliant on harmful substances or behaviors to function. The first step in healing this dependency is detoxification, which involves removing the addictive substance from the body and managing withdrawal symptoms. This process can be challenging and may require medical supervision, but it is essential for breaking the cycle of addiction and beginning the journey toward recovery.

Once detoxification is complete, ongoing treatment is crucial to support the body's healing process. Physical therapy and other rehabilitation services can aid in restoring the body's strength and functionality. It's important to approach treatment with a holistic mindset, addressing not only the physical aspects of addiction but also the psychological and emotional factors that contribute to dependency.

Adopting healthy habits is another vital component of overcoming physical dependency. Regular exercise plays a significant role in recovery, as it helps to improve mood, reduce stress, and enhance overall physical health. Activities such as walking, running, sports, and strength training can provide structure and a sense of accomplishment, which are beneficial during the recovery process. Exercise also releases endorphins, the body's natural feel-good chemicals, which can help counteract the negative feelings often associated with withdrawal and recovery.

Balanced nutrition and adequate rest are equally important in nurturing the body back to health. Addiction can deplete the body of essential nutrients, so it's crucial to consume a diet rich in vitamins, minerals, and other nutrients to aid in physical recovery. Eating a variety of fruits, vegetables, lean proteins, and whole grains can help rebuild the body's strength and improve overall well-being. Additionally, getting enough rest is essential for healing, as sleep allows the body to repair itself and restore energy levels. Adequate rest also gives the mind the strength to utilize its will power. By committing to a healthy lifestyle, individuals can restore their physical health and build the resilience needed to maintain long-term recovery.

Withdrawal symptoms and cravings are among the most challenging components of overcoming physical dependency. Symptoms can include nausea, sweating, shaking, anxiety, depression, and intense cravings for the substance. These physical manifestations can be so overwhelming that individuals may feel compelled to return to their addictive behavior simply to alleviate the discomfort. The intensity of withdrawal often varies depending on the substance and the duration of use, but it consistently poses a significant barrier to recovery.

The Path to Renewal

The journey to overcoming addiction is not a passive one. It requires active participation and relentless determination. The process of cleansing and renewing the mind, body, and spirit is a holistic approach that addresses all facets of addiction.

"Break Every Chain": A Movement of Liberation

"Break Every Chain" is more than just this book; it is a movement dedicated to sending addictions to the grave, before they send us to the grave. This movement draws on the power of God, His healing power, and merciful ways. By embracing this divine strength, individuals struggling with addiction can find hope and a path to recovery. The movement seeks to empower people by showing them that they are not alone in their struggle, and that with faith and determination, they can overcome the chains of addiction.

The movement is deeply rooted in God, drawing inspiration from Biblical verses such as Isaiah 58:6, "Is not this the fast that I have chosen? to loose the bands of wickedness, to undo the heavy burdens, and to let the oppressed go free, and that ye break every yoke?" and John 8:36, "If the Son therefore shall make you free, ye shall be free indeed". These scriptures underscore the promise of liberation and serve as a powerful reminder that freedom from addiction is possible through the grace of God. They highlight the compassionate and liberating nature of divine intervention, encouraging those battling addiction to seek solace and strength in their faith.

Jesus, often referred to as the Lion of Judah, is about healing the sick, and addiction is undoubtedly a sickness that afflicts many. His teachings and actions exemplify the profound healing that is available to all who seek it. In the context of addiction, His message of hope and recovery resonates deeply, offering a beacon of light to those in the darkest of times. The belief that the Lion of Judah will break every chain is central to the movement, providing a powerful symbol of strength and deliverance.

The principles found in these verses can be directly applied to addiction and recovery, reminding us that we are not alone in our struggle and that there is a greater power ready to help us break free. By integrating these spiritual insights into our recovery journey, we can draw strength and inspiration to persevere. The journey to overcoming addiction is arduous, but with the support of a faith-based community and the guidance of scripture, individuals can find the resilience to reclaim their lives. "Break Every Chain" is more than a call to action; it is a testament to the transformative power of faith and the unwavering belief that freedom from addiction is attainable for everyone.

The Power of Effort and Perseverance

While the journey to overcoming addiction may seem daunting, it is entirely within our ability to conquer it. This guide is crafted to provide guidance and support along the way, offering strategies and insights to navigate the challenges of recovery. However, the ultimate success of this journey hinges on your determination, effort, and perseverance. Every step forward, no matter how small, marks a significant victory in reclaiming control over your life from the grip of addiction.

It is crucial not to attempt this journey alone. Seeking the support of God and a strong community of peers and mentors can make a profound difference in your recovery. God's presence and guidance offer spiritual strength and comfort, providing a foundation of faith to draw upon during times of trial. Additionally, a supportive group can offer understanding, encouragement, and accountability, essential elements in sustaining long-term sobriety and healing.

Throughout this process, you will encounter tests and moments of struggle. These challenges are normal parts of the journey toward recovery, each presenting an opportunity for growth and resilience. Embracing the support of others and remaining steadfast in your commitment to change will empower you to overcome obstacles and continue moving forward. With faith, determination, and the backing of a caring community, you can navigate the path to freedom from addiction and build a fulfilling, sober life.

The Goal of Freedom

Freedom from addiction is the ultimate goal. It is a state of being where we are no longer controlled by our dependencies but instead live a life of purpose and fulfillment. Achieving this freedom requires unwavering commitment and the courage to face and overcome our challenges.

Conquering All Forms of Addiction

This movement is committed to conquering all forms of addiction, whether it be drugs, alcohol, sex, pornography, food, gambling, video games, shopping, marijuana, devices, the internet, caffeine, or any other dependency. The message is clear: no addiction is too powerful to overcome.

Conclusion

The journey to overcoming addiction is a profound transformation that demands a holistic approach, addressing the mind, body, and spirit. While the path is challenging, the promise of freedom is worth every effort. "Break Every Chain" is a call to action, urging us to reclaim our lives from the clutches of addiction. By committing to this journey and drawing on spiritual, mental, and physical resources, we can break free and live a life of purpose and fulfillment. Let us rise to the challenge, break every chain, and send addiction to the grave.

First Round of Execution

Exercise 1: Identifying Your Addictions

Instructions: Write down the specific addictions you are struggling with. Be as detailed as possible.

The Addictions:

Exercise 2: Understanding the Impact

Instructions: Reflect on how your addiction has affected various aspects of your life. Fill in the table below.

Aspect of Life   Negative Impact

Physical Health

Mental Health

Relationships

Work/School

Finances

Exercise 3. Recognizing the Problem

Exercise 3: Self-Assessment Quiz

Instructions: Answer the following questions to assess the severity of your addiction.

1. How often do you engage in your addictive behaviors?

2. Have you tried to stop and failed?

3. Does your addiction interfere with daily responsibilities?

4. Do you experience withdrawal symptoms?

Score: [ ] Mild [ ] Moderate [ ] Severe

Exercise 4: Reflecting on Your Habits

Instructions: Write a reflection about when and why you engage in your addictive behaviors. Consider the emotions, situations, or people involved.

Reflection:

Preparing for Change

Exercise 5: Setting Realistic Goals

Instructions: Set three specific, achievable goals for your recovery. Break them down into smaller steps if necessary.

1. **Goal 1:**

   o   Steps:

2. **Goal 2:**

   o   Steps:

3. **Goal 3:**

   o   Steps:

Exercise 6: Building Your Support System

Instructions: List the people you can rely on for support. Describe how each person can help you.

Support Network:

Name Relationship How They Can Help

Exercise 7: Practicing Meditation

Instructions: Set aside time each day for scripture reading and to practice meditation. Use the space below to schedule your daily meditation times.

Meditation Schedule:

Day	Time	Time	Time
Sunday			
Monday			
Tuesday			
Wednesday			
Thursday			
Friday			

Exercise 8: Creating an Exercise Routine

Instructions: Plan a weekly exercise routine. Include different types of physical activities you enjoy. Give Yourself a minimum one day of rest.

Exercise Routine:

Day	Activity	Duration
Sunday		
Monday		
Tuesday		
Wednesday		
Thursday		
Friday		

Exercise 9: Exploring Healthy Hobbies

Instructions: List hobbies and activities you are interested in or would like to try. Set goals for incorporating them into your routine.

Hobbies and Activities:

Hobby/Activity Goal Timeline

Avoiding Triggers and Relapse

Exercise 10: Identifying Your Triggers

Instructions: Identify your triggers by filling in the table below. Include specific situations, people, or emotions that lead to your addictive behavior.

Triggers:

Trigger Situation/Person/Emotion Response

Exercise 11: Developing Coping Strategies

Instructions: Develop coping strategies for each trigger. List healthy alternatives and coping mechanisms.

Coping Strategies:

Building a Healthy Lifestyle

Exercise 12: Nutrition and Meal Planning

Instructions: Plan a week's worth of healthy meals. Focus on balanced nutrition to support your recovery.

Meal Plan:

Day	Breakfast	Lunch	Dinner	Snacks
Monday				
Tuesday				
Wednesday				
Thursday				
Friday				
Saturday				
Sunday				

Exercise 13: Establishing a Sleep Routine

Instructions: Create a bedtime routine to improve sleep quality. Include relaxing activities before bed. Limit electronic devices at least 30 minutes prior to sleep.

Pre-bedtime Routine:

Bedtime	Wake up Time
Sunday:	
Monday:	
Tuesday:	
Wednesday:	
Thursday:	
Friday:	
Saturday:	

Exercise 14: Strengthening Social Connections

Instructions: Identify ways to strengthen your social

connections. Plan activities to engage with supportive people.

Social Activities:

Person/Group Activity Frequency

Exercise 15: Setting Healthy Boundaries

Instructions: List four People/ Places/ Things you will avoid

1.)

2.)

3.)

4.)

How will you avoid these things?

Staying Motivated

Exercise 16: Celebrating Milestones

Instructions: Set milestones for your recovery and plan how you will celebrate each achievement.

Milestones and Celebrations:

Milestone Celebration Date Achieved

Exercise 17: Maintaining Long-Term Recovery

Instructions: Reflect on strategies that have helped you and plan how to continue using them in the future.

Long-Term Recovery Plan:

Exercise 18: Joining Support Groups

Instructions: Find and join support groups or online communities. Note meeting times and how to participate.

Support Groups:

Group/Community Meeting Time How to Join

5 Day Reflection

During the next five days, take the time to complete your exercise reflections. This period is an opportunity to step back and evaluate your progress so far. You can choose to rest from some of your disciplines to give yourself a break, or you can continue any that you find particularly beneficial. The primary goal during these days is to review what worked well and what didn't, as you prepare to make necessary adjustments for the upcoming forty days—the second round of execution.

As you reflect, focus on identifying the strengths and weaknesses of your current approach. What exercises or strategies yielded positive results? Which ones fell short of your expectations, and why? Be honest with yourself about your successes and setbacks. This self-awareness will be crucial in tailoring your plan moving forward. Consider journaling your thoughts and feelings during this period to gain deeper insights into your journey and to have a record to look back on.

Use this time to recalibrate and re-energize. Reflecting on your experiences can provide valuable lessons and renewed motivation. Think about how you can enhance your strategies and what additional support you might need. By thoroughly reviewing and understanding your progress, you will be better equipped to tackle the next phase of the program with confidence and a clear, focused plan. This review period is not just a pause but a vital step in ensuring your continued growth and success in breaking free from addiction.

You have 5 Days to fill out pages 46-66. Give yourself time each day to work on it. Reflect on how you did with the exercises.

Reflection Start Date: _____

Date 5 Days from Reflection Start Date: _____

Journal Prompts to Review the First 18 Exercises

1. **Exercise Reflection**:

   - o Which exercise did you find most challenging, and why? How did you overcome these challenges?

2. **Personal Growth**:

   - o How have the exercises contributed to your personal growth? Provide specific examples.

3. **Emotional Response**:

   - o What emotions did you experience while completing the exercises? How did you manage these emotions?

4. **Successes and Milestones**:

   o   What successes or milestones did you achieve
       during the exercises? How did you celebrate
       them?

5. **Learning Outcomes**:

   o   What are the most important lessons you have
       learned from these exercises?

6. **Support System**:

   o   How did your support system contribute to your
       progress with the exercises? Provide specific
       instances where their support made a difference.

7. **Strategies and Tools**:

    o   What strategies or tools from the exercises have
        been most effective for you? How will you
        continue to use them?

8. **Challenges and Obstacles**:

    o   What were the biggest obstacles you faced during
        these exercises, and how did you address them?

9. **Coping Mechanisms**:

    o   How have your coping mechanisms evolved since
        starting the exercises? What new techniques have
        you adopted?

10. **Mental and Physical Changes**:

   o   Have you noticed any mental or physical changes
       since beginning the exercises? Describe these
       changes.

11. **Mindset Shifts**:

   o   How has your mindset shifted as a result of
       completing the exercises? What new perspectives
       have you gained?

12. **Consistency and Discipline**:

   o   How consistent and disciplined were you in
       completing the exercises? What motivated you to
       stay on track?

13. **Exercise Revisions**:

   o   Are there any exercises you would approach
       differently? How will you modify your approach?

14. **Connection to Faith**:

   o   How have the exercises strengthened your faith or
       spiritual life? Provide specific examples.

15. **Impact on Daily Life**:

   o   How have the exercises impacted your daily life
       and routines? What changes have you
       implemented?

16. **Peer Insights**:

   o   What insights or advice from peers or your
       support group have been particularly helpful
       during the exercises?

17. **Future Application**:

   o   How do you plan to apply what you've learned
       from these exercises to future challenges or goals?

18. **Final Thoughts**:

   o   What are your overall thoughts on the first 18
       exercises? How do you feel about your progress
       and what lies ahead in the program?

Modifications

As you prepare for the second round of execution, take the time to revisit and modify exercises 5-18 if necessary, below. Reflect on what didn't work in the first round and make the necessary adjustments to improve your approach. This might involve changing the timing of certain exercises, incorporating additional support mechanisms, or refining your strategies for managing triggers and stress. If certain exercises were effective and yielded positive results, keep them unchanged. The goal is to optimize your plan to ensure that the second round of execution is even more effective in helping you overcome addiction.

The second round of execution is crucial as it represents a deeper commitment to fully eliminating your addiction. By this stage, new habits will have started to form, and you will notice significant changes in your behavior and mindset. Embrace this transformation and continue to build on it, reinforcing your new identity in Christ. This phase is about solidifying the progress you've made and pushing forward with renewed determination and faith. Trust in the process, stay committed to the exercises, and rely on your support system. With each step, you are becoming a new person, free from the chains of addiction and empowered by your spiritual growth and resilience.

Second Round of Execution

Day 55 marks the beginning of the second round of execution, a pivotal phase in your journey to overcome addiction. With the insights gained from the first round and any modifications you've made, you are now better prepared to tackle the exercises with renewed focus and determination. You will only be doing exercises 5-18 this go around. This is crunch time; it's about deepening your commitment and fully engaging with each exercise to eliminate any remaining toxic traits and negative behaviors. Approach this phase with the mindset of transformation, knowing that each step you take brings you closer to complete recovery.

As you progress through the exercises again, emphasize re-programming your mind. This involves not only breaking old habits but also cultivating new, positive ones. Utilize the strategies and tools that worked well during the first round, and implement the adjustments you've identified to address any weaknesses. Stay vigilant and mindful of your thoughts and actions, constantly reinforcing the new patterns you are establishing. Remember, this is not just about going through the motions but about intentional, purposeful change that reflects your commitment to a healthier, addiction-free life.

This second round of execution is a critical period for solidifying the changes you've made and ensuring they become a permanent part of your life. As you eliminate toxic traits, you are also nurturing your new identity in Christ, who strengthens you. Each exercise is a step toward complete mental, emotional, and spiritual renewal. Stay focused, keep your support system close, and continue to lean on your faith. This phase is challenging, but it's also incredibly rewarding. By the end of this round, you will be significantly closer to breaking every chain and fully embracing the new, empowered person you are becoming.

Start Date, Second Round: _____

40 Days After Start Date of Second Round

Completion Date: _____

Preparing for Change

Exercise 5: Setting Realistic Goals

Instructions: Set three specific, achievable goals for your recovery. Break them down into smaller steps if necessary.

1. **Goal 1:**

   o Steps:

2. **Goal 2:**

   o Steps:

3. **Goal 3:**

   o Steps:

Exercise 6: Building Your Support System

Instructions: List the people you can rely on for support. Describe how each person can help you.

Support Network:

Name Relationship How They Can Help

Exercise 7: Practicing Meditation

Instructions: Set aside time each day for scripture reading and to practice meditation. Use the space below to schedule your daily meditation times.

Meditation Schedule:

Day	Time	Time	Time
Sunday			
Monday			
Tuesday			
Wednesday			
Thursday			
Friday			

Exercise 8: Creating an Exercise Routine

Instructions: Plan a weekly exercise routine. Include different types of physical activities you enjoy. Give Yourself a minimum one day of rest.

Exercise Routine:

Day	Activity	Duration
Sunday		
Monday		
Tuesday		
Wednesday		
Thursday		
Friday		

Exercise 9: Exploring Healthy Hobbies

Instructions: List hobbies and activities you are interested in or would like to try. Set goals for incorporating them into your routine.

Hobbies and Activities:

Hobby/Activity Goal Timeline

Avoiding Triggers and Relapse

Exercise 10: Identifying Your Triggers

Instructions: Identify your triggers by filling in the table below. Include specific situations, people, or emotions that lead to your addictive behavior.

Triggers:

Trigger Situation/Person/Emotion Response

Exercise 11: Developing Coping Strategies

Instructions: Develop coping strategies for each trigger. List healthy alternatives and coping mechanisms.

Coping Strategies:

Building a Healthy Lifestyle

Exercise 12: Nutrition and Meal Planning

Instructions: Plan a week's worth of healthy meals. Focus on balanced nutrition to support your recovery.

Meal Plan:

Day	Breakfast	Lunch	Dinner	Snacks
Monday				
Tuesday				
Wednesday				
Thursday				
Friday				
Saturday				
Sunday				

Exercise 13: Establishing a Sleep Routine

Instructions: Create a bedtime routine to improve sleep quality. Include relaxing activities before bed. Limit electronic devices at least 30 minutes prior to sleep.

Pre-bedtime Routine:

	Bedtime	Wake up Time
Sunday:		
Monday:		
Tuesday:		
Wednesday:		
Thursday:		
Friday:		
Saturday:		

Exercise 14: Strengthening Social Connections

Instructions: Identify ways to strengthen your social

connections. Plan activities to engage with supportive people.

Social Activities:

Person/Group Activity Frequency

Exercise 15: Setting Healthy Boundaries

Instructions: List four People/ Places/ Things you will avoid

1.)

2.)

3.)

4.)

How will you avoid these things?

Staying Motivated

Exercise 16: Celebrating Milestones

Instructions: Set milestones for your recovery and plan how you will celebrate each achievement.

Milestones and Celebrations:

Milestone Celebration Date Achieved

Exercise 17: Maintaining Long-Term Recovery

Instructions: Reflect on strategies that have helped you and plan how to continue using them in the future.

Long-Term Recovery Plan:

Exercise 18: Joining Support Groups

Instructions: Find and join support groups or online communities. Note meeting times and how to participate.

Support Groups:

Group/Community Meeting Time How to Join

Day 55: Second Round of Execution

Day 55 marks the beginning of the second round of execution, a pivotal phase in your journey to overcome addiction. With the insights gained from the first round and any modifications you've made, you are now better prepared to tackle the exercises with renewed focus and determination. You will only be doing exercises 5-18 this go around. This is crunch time; it's about deepening your commitment and fully engaging with each exercise to eliminate any remaining toxic traits and negative behaviors. Approach this phase with the mindset of transformation, knowing that each step you take brings you closer to complete recovery.

As you progress through the exercises again, emphasize re-programming your mind. This involves not only breaking old habits but also cultivating new, positive ones. Utilize the strategies and tools that worked well during the first round, and implement the adjustments you've identified to address any weaknesses. Stay vigilant and mindful of your thoughts and actions, constantly reinforcing the new patterns you are establishing. Remember, this is not just about going through the motions but about intentional, purposeful change that reflects your commitment to a healthier, addiction-free life.

This second round of execution is a critical period for solidifying the changes you've made and ensuring they become a permanent part of your life. As you eliminate toxic traits, you are also nurturing your new identity in Christ, who strengthens you. Each exercise is a step toward complete mental, emotional, and spiritual renewal. Stay focused, keep your support system close, and continue to lean on your faith. This phase is challenging, but it's also incredibly rewarding. By the end of this round, you will be significantly closer to breaking every chain and fully embracing the new, empowered person you are becoming.

Start Date, Second Round: _____

40 Days After Start Date of Second Round

Completion Date: _____

Day 95- 100

Reflection Questions

1.) How have you grown spiritually, mentally, and emotionally throughout this 100-day journey?

2.) What were the most significant challenges you faced, and how did you overcome them?

3.) Reflecting on the exercises and activities, which ones had the most positive impact on your journey to overcome addiction?

4.) In what ways have your relationships with others improved as a result of your commitment to breaking free from addiction?

5.) How has your perspective on life and your future changed since beginning the program?

6.) What new habits have you developed that support your ongoing recovery and personal growth?

7.) How has your faith or spiritual beliefs strengthened during this process?

8.) What have you learned about yourself—your strengths, weaknesses, and resilience?

9.) How do you plan to maintain the progress you've made and continue growing after completing the program?

10.) Looking back, what advice would you give to someone else who is beginning their journey to overcome addiction?

You Did It!

Congratulations on completing the Break Every Chain Freedom From All Addictions 100 Day Re-Program! Your dedication and perseverance throughout this journey are truly commendable. By committing to this program, you have taken a significant step towards breaking free from the grip of addiction and reclaiming your life.

Throughout these 100 days, you have experienced numerous benefits. You have gained practical strategies and spiritual insights that empower you to overcome addictive behaviors. You have cultivated new habits and coping mechanisms that support your ongoing recovery. Most importantly, you have discovered a renewed sense of hope and purpose as you walk the path towards healing.

As you reflect on your achievements, consider the positive changes you have witnessed—mentally, emotionally, and spiritually. Your commitment to self-improvement not only benefits you but also inspires others around you. We encourage you to share your success with friends and loved ones, inviting them to embark on their own journey of freedom from addiction.

Remember, overcoming addiction is a continuous journey. Whether you choose to repeat this program for further growth or support others in their recovery, your experience and encouragement can make a profound difference. We applaud your courage and determination, and we celebrate every victory, big or small, on your path to a life free from addiction.

Call Log

Maintaining a call log plays a crucial role in the journey to overcome addiction, functioning as a fundamental tool for accountability and support. By diligently documenting calls related to recovery efforts, individuals can systematically track their progress, commitments made to support groups or sponsors, and pivotal discussions about their treatment plans. This structured record not only fosters organizational clarity but also serves as a reliable reference for reviewing challenges overcome, breakthroughs achieved, and the continuous support received from others. In the context of addiction recovery, where consistency and transparency are pivotal to success, a call log becomes an indispensable asset for fostering discipline, maintaining accountability, and ensuring sustained focus on the path toward lasting recovery and personal growth.

Moreover, a well-maintained call log empowers individuals in addiction recovery by providing tangible evidence of their efforts and milestones achieved over time. It allows for reflection on the journey's progression, reinforcing positive changes and highlighting areas where additional support or adjustments may be needed. By capturing both successes and setbacks in a structured manner, individuals can gain deeper insights into their own recovery process, enabling them to make informed decisions and stay committed to their goals. Ultimately, the disciplined practice of maintaining a call log not only supports individual accountability but also strengthens the foundation for a resilient and transformative recovery journey.

Date/ Time:

Name of Caller/Recipient:

Purpose:

Outcome [Summary of what was discussed or achieved]:

Next Steps: [Any actions or follow-ups required]

Date/ Time:

Name of Caller/Recipient:

Purpose:

Outcome [Summary of what was discussed or achieved]:

Next Steps: [Any actions or follow-ups required]

Date/ Time:

Name of Caller/Recipient:

Purpose:

Outcome [Summary of what was discussed or achieved]:

Next Steps: [Any actions or follow-ups required]

Date/ Time:

Name of Caller/Recipient:

Purpose:

Outcome [Summary of what was discussed or achieved]:

Next Steps: [Any actions or follow-ups required]

Date/ Time:

Name of Caller/Recipient:

Purpose:

Outcome [Summary of what was discussed or achieved]:

Next Steps: [Any actions or follow-ups required]

Date/ Time:

Name of Caller/Recipient:

Purpose:

Outcome [Summary of what was discussed or achieved]:

Next Steps: [Any actions or follow-ups required]

Date/ Time:

Name of Caller/Recipient:

Purpose:

Outcome [Summary of what was discussed or achieved]:

Next Steps: [Any actions or follow-ups required]

Date/ Time:

Name of Caller/Recipient:

Purpose:

Outcome [Summary of what was discussed or achieved]:

Next Steps: [Any actions or follow-ups required]

Date/ Time:

Name of Caller/Recipient:

Purpose:

Outcome [Summary of what was discussed or achieved]:

Next Steps: [Any actions or follow-ups required]

Date/ Time:

Name of Caller/Recipient:

Purpose:

Outcome [Summary of what was discussed or achieved]:

Next Steps: [Any actions or follow-ups required]

Date/ Time:

Name of Caller/Recipient:

Purpose:

Outcome [Summary of what was discussed or achieved]:

Next Steps: [Any actions or follow-ups required]

Date/ Time:

Name of Caller/Recipient:

Purpose:

Outcome [Summary of what was discussed or achieved]:

Next Steps: [Any actions or follow-ups required]

Date/ Time:

Name of Caller/Recipient:

Purpose:

Outcome [Summary of what was discussed or achieved]:

Next Steps: [Any actions or follow-ups required]

Date/ Time:

Name of Caller/Recipient:

Purpose:

Outcome [Summary of what was discussed or achieved]:

Next Steps: [Any actions or follow-ups required]

Date/ Time:

Name of Caller/Recipient:

Purpose:

Outcome [Summary of what was discussed or achieved]:

Next Steps: [Any actions or follow-ups required]

Date/ Time:

Name of Caller/Recipient:

Purpose:

Outcome [Summary of what was discussed or achieved]:

Next Steps: [Any actions or follow-ups required]

Date/ Time:

Name of Caller/Recipient:

Purpose:

Outcome [Summary of what was discussed or achieved]:

Next Steps: [Any actions or follow-ups required]

Date/ Time:

Name of Caller/Recipient:

Purpose:

Outcome [Summary of what was discussed or achieved]:

Next Steps: [Any actions or follow-ups required]

Date/ Time:

Date/ Time:

Name of Caller/Recipient:

Purpose:

Outcome [Summary of what was discussed or achieved]:

Next Steps: [Any actions or follow-ups required]

Date/ Time:

Name of Caller/Recipient:

Purpose:

Outcome [Summary of what was discussed or achieved]:

Next Steps: [Any actions or follow-ups required]

Date/ Time:

Name of Caller/Recipient:

Purpose:

Outcome [Summary of what was discussed or achieved]:

Next Steps: [Any actions or follow-ups required]

Date/ Time:

Name of Caller/Recipient:

Purpose:

Outcome [Summary of what was discussed or achieved]:

Next Steps: [Any actions or follow-ups required]

Date/ Time:

Name of Caller/Recipient:

Purpose:

Outcome [Summary of what was discussed or achieved]:

Next Steps: [Any actions or follow-ups required]

Date/ Time:

Name of Caller/Recipient:

Purpose:

Outcome [Summary of what was discussed or achieved]:

Next Steps: [Any actions or follow-ups required]

Date/ Time:

Name of Caller/Recipient:

Purpose:

Outcome [Summary of what was discussed or achieved]:

Next Steps: [Any actions or follow-ups required]

Date/ Time:

Name of Caller/Recipient:

Purpose:

Outcome [Summary of what was discussed or achieved]:

Next Steps: [Any actions or follow-ups required]

Date/ Time:

Name of Caller/Recipient:

Purpose:

Outcome [Summary of what was discussed or achieved]:

Next Steps: [Any actions or follow-ups required]

Date/ Time:

Name of Caller/Recipient:

Purpose:

Outcome [Summary of what was discussed or achieved]:

Next Steps: [Any actions or follow-ups required]

Name of Caller/Recipient:

Date/ Time:

Name of Caller/Recipient:

Purpose:

Outcome [Summary of what was discussed or achieved]:

Next Steps: [Any actions or follow-ups required]

Date/ Time:

Name of Caller/Recipient:

Purpose:

Outcome [Summary of what was discussed or achieved]:

Next Steps: [Any actions or follow-ups required]

Date/ Time:

Name of Caller/Recipient:

Purpose:

Outcome [Summary of what was discussed or achieved]:

Next Steps: [Any actions or follow-ups required]

Date/ Time:

Name of Caller/Recipient:

Purpose:

Outcome [Summary of what was discussed or achieved]:

Next Steps: [Any actions or follow-ups required]

Date/ Time:

Name of Caller/Recipient:

Purpose:

Outcome [Summary of what was discussed or achieved]:

Next Steps: [Any actions or follow-ups required]

Date/ Time:

Name of Caller/Recipient:

Purpose:

Outcome [Summary of what was discussed or achieved]:

Next Steps: [Any actions or follow-ups required]

Date/ Time:

Name of Caller/Recipient:

Purpose:

Outcome [Summary of what was discussed or achieved]:

Next Steps: [Any actions or follow-ups required]

Date/ Time:

Name of Caller/Recipient:

Purpose:

Outcome [Summary of what was discussed or achieved]:

Next Steps: [Any actions or follow-ups required]

Date/ Time:

Name of Caller/Recipient:

Purpose:

Outcome [Summary of what was discussed or achieved]:

Next Steps: [Any actions or follow-ups required]

Date/ Time:

Name of Caller/Recipient:

Purpose:

Outcome [Summary of what was discussed or achieved]:

Next Steps: [Any actions or follow-ups required]

Date/ Time:

Name of Caller/Recipient:

Purpose:

Outcome [Summary of what was discussed or achieved]:

Next Steps: [Any actions or follow-ups required]

Date/ Time:

Name of Caller/Recipient:

Purpose:

Outcome [Summary of what was discussed or achieved]:

Next Steps: [Any actions or follow-ups required]

In the Event of Relapse

In the journey to overcome addiction, it is essential to understand that relapse does not signify failure. If you experience a slip-up, don't view it as the end of your progress. Instead, think of it as a temporary setback. Relapse can happen, but it is crucial not to let it deter you or make you feel defeated. A momentary lapse does not erase all the hard work and progress you have made. Jump back on the horse and keep riding, knowing that every step forward, even after a fall, is a victory in itself.

Addiction recovery is not an all-or-nothing endeavor. The path to healing is often winding and filled with challenges. It's important to approach each day with a mindset of resilience and self-compassion. If you slip up, resist the urge to beat yourself up or dwell on the mistake. Instead, acknowledge what happened, understand the circumstances that led to the relapse, and use that insight to strengthen your resolve. Remember, you are human, and setbacks are a natural part of any journey. Dust yourself off, learn from the experience, and try again with renewed determination.

Every time you get back up after a fall, you build greater strength and resilience. Each attempt to overcome addiction, even after a relapse, brings you closer to lasting recovery. The most important thing is to stay committed to your goals and believe in your capacity to change. Surround yourself with supportive individuals who can help you navigate these challenges and remind you of your progress. Keep your focus on the long-term journey, not the occasional setbacks, and trust that with perseverance and support, you can break free from addiction and reclaim your life.

Beneficial Bible Passages

<u>1 Corinthians 10:13</u> - There hath no temptation taken you but such as is common to man: but God is faithful, who will not suffer you to be tempted above that ye are able; but will with the temptation also make a way to escape, that ye may be able to bear it.

<u>1 Peter 5:8</u> - Be sober, be vigilant; because your adversary the devil, as a roaring lion, walketh about, seeking whom he may devour:

<u>James 1:12-15</u> - Blessed is the man that endureth temptation: for when he is tried, he shall receive the crown of life, which the Lord hath promised to them that love him. Let no man say when he is tempted, I am tempted of God: for God cannot be tempted with evil, neither tempteth he any man: But every man is tempted, when he is drawn away of his own lust, and enticed. Then when lust hath conceived, it bringeth forth sin: and sin, when it is finished, bringeth forth death.

<u>1 John 2:16</u> - For all that is in the world, the lust of the flesh, and the lust of the eyes, and the pride of life, is not of the Father, but is of the world.

<u>1 Corinthians 15:33</u> - Be not deceived: evil communications corrupt good manners.

<u>1 Peter 5:10</u> - But the God of all grace, who hath called us unto

his eternal glory by Christ Jesus, after that ye have suffered a while, make you perfect, stablish, strengthen, settle you.

James 4:7 - Submit yourselves therefore to God. Resist the devil, and he will flee from you.

1 Corinthians 6:12 - All things are lawful unto me, but all things are not expedient: all things are lawful for me, but I will not be brought under the power of any.

Galatians 5:19-21 - Now the works of the flesh are manifest, which are these; Adultery, fornication, uncleanness, lasciviousness, Idolatry, witchcraft, hatred, variance, emulations, wrath, strife, seditions, heresies, Envyings, murders, drunkenness, revellings, and such like: of the which I tell you before, as I have also told *you* in time past, that they which do such things shall not inherit the kingdom of God.

1 Peter 2:11 - Dearly beloved, I beseech you as strangers and pilgrims, abstain from fleshly lusts, which war against the soul;

Proverbs 20:1 - Wine is a mocker, strong drink is raging: and whosoever is deceived thereby is not wise.

Psalms 50:15 - And call upon me in the day of trouble: I will deliver thee, and thou shalt glorify me.

Romans 13:14 - But put ye on the Lord Jesus Christ, and make not provision for the flesh, to fulfil the lusts thereof.

Romans 5:3-5 - And not only so, but we glory in tribulations also: knowing that tribulation worketh patience; And patience, experience; and experience, hope: And hope maketh not ashamed; because the love of God is shed abroad in our hearts by the Holy Ghost which is given unto us.

Matthew 6:13 - And lead us not into temptation, but deliver us from evil: For thine is the kingdom, and the power, and the glory, for ever. Amen.

Proverbs 6:27 - Can a man take fire in his bosom, and his clothes not be burned?

1 Corinthians 6:18 - Flee fornication. Every sin that a man doeth is without the body; but he that committeth fornication sinneth against his own body.

Galatians 5:16 - This I say then, Walk in the Spirit, and ye shall not fulfil the lust of the flesh.

John 8:36 - If the Son therefore shall make you free, ye shall be free indeed.

2 Peter 2:19 - While they promise them liberty, they themselves are the servants of corruption: for of whom a man is overcome, of the same is he brought in bondage.

About the Author

Karajah Yashar is a distinguished graduate of Rutgers University, whose counseling career spans over two decades. With extensive experience in working with both youth and adults, Karajah has dedicated his professional life to supporting those struggling with addiction. His work has taken him to some of the most challenging environments, including counseling among incarcerated men, military veterans, and the homeless population. Through his compassionate and skilled approach, Karajah has provided crucial guidance and support to countless individuals on their path to recovery.

Driven by a profound understanding of the devastating impact addiction can have on individuals, families, and communities, Karajah is deeply committed to combating this pervasive issue. His determination to neutralize the stinging effect of addiction is evident in his tireless efforts and unwavering dedication. Karajah's holistic and empathetic approach to counseling has made him a respected and influential figure in the field of addiction recovery, as he continues to make a meaningful difference in the lives of those he serves.